JUMP

JOURNAL FOR UNDERSTANDING MATHEMATICAL PRINCIPLES

Eliza Akana

Jonelle Flight

Suzanne Forbes

Ann Watanabe

Common Core Education, Inc.

Maui, Hawaii

2nd Edition

Second Edition

ISBN-13: 9780615814445

ISBN-10: 0615814441

Printed in the United States of America

Cover design by Jessica Matsumoto

This **JUMP** belongs to:

_____

Teacher:

_____

Grade:

_____

School:

_____

Signal Words

Signal Words are important words that tell you what you need to do on each journal page.

Draw	Draw a picture or a model.	Draw
Label	Give a name to something you have drawn or written.	Label
Write	Write words or numbers.	Write
Solve	Find the solution or the answer.	Solve
Explain	Put your thinking into complete sentences.	Explain
Measure	Use a math measuring tool.	Measure

Mathematician

Draw a picture of yourself and label yourself a **mathematician**.

Draw and Label

Explain what makes you a **mathematician**.

Explain

Maria bought 21 bananas to make pies. Josh gave her 13 more bananas. Maria used 27 bananas for the pies. How many bananas does Maria have left? Draw a picture. Write an equation. Use a ? for the unknown number. Solve this word problem.

Draw

Write

Solve

Jamal has some baseball cards. He gets 37 more baseball cards for his birthday. Now he has 96 baseball cards. How many cards did Jamal have before his birthday? **Draw** a picture. **Write** an equation. Use a ? for the unknown number. **Solve** this word problem.

Draw

Write

Solve

Lin had 99¢ in her pocket. She bought a pink balloon at the party store. Now she has 24¢ left. How much did the balloon cost? Draw a picture. Write an equation. Use a ? for the unknown number. Solve this word problem.

Draw

Write

Solve

There are 80 insects on an apple tree. Thirty-seven insects are ladybugs, and the rest are bumble bees. How many bumble bees are on the apple tree? Draw a picture. Write an equation. Use a ? for the unknown number. Solve this word problem.

Draw

Write

Solve

4

Omar has 11 books to place on two shelves. How many books can he put on the top shelf, and how many books can he put on the bottom shelf? Write an equation. Use a ? for the unknown number. Draw a picture.

Write

Draw

Think of a different way that Omar can organize the books. Write an equation. Use a ? for the unknown number. Draw a picture.

Write

Draw

Ian has 12 more stickers on his skateboard than Nina. Nina has 19 stickers on her skateboard. How many stickers does Ian have on his skateboard? Draw a picture. Write an equation. Use a ? for the unknown number. Solve this word problem.

Draw

Write

Solve

CCSS.2.OA.1—F

Val has 12 fewer stickers on her skateboard than Lola. Lola has 19 stickers on her skateboard. How many stickers does Val have on her skateboard? Draw a picture. Write an equation. Use a ? for the unknown number. Solve this word problem.

Draw

Write

Solve

Keesha's house has five more windows than Quinten's house. Keesha's house has 16 windows. How many windows does Quinten's house have? Draw a picture. Write an equation. Use a ? for the unknown number. Solve this word problem.

Draw

Write

Solve

8

CCSS.2.OA.1—H

© Common Core Education, Inc.

Jordan's house has six fewer windows than Jacob's house. Jordan's house has 15 windows. How many windows does Jacob's house have? Draw a picture. Write an equation. Use a ? for the unknown number. Solve this word problem.

Draw

Write

Solve

Write all of the strategies you have learned that help students memorize their addition facts. **Explain** which of these strategies works best for you.

Write

Explain

CCSS.2.OA.2

Write an even number that is less than 20. **Draw** a picture that proves your number is even. **Explain** why your number is even.

Write

Draw

Explain

_____

_____

_____

_____

_____

Write an odd number that is less than 20. **Draw** a picture that proves your number is odd. **Explain** why your number is odd.

Write

Draw

Explain

Draw a rectangular array that has a sum of 18. **Write** an equation for your array.

Draw

Write

There are five hundred nine students in a school. Draw a model of this number using hundreds, tens, and ones. Write the number in base-ten numerals. Explain the value of each digit.

Draw

Write

Explain

CCSS.2.NBT.1

Draw a model to show how many bundles of ten there are in 100. Write how many dimes make a dollar. Explain how a dime is like a bundle of 10.

Draw

Write

Explain

Write how many hundreds there are in the number 800.

> Write

Write how many ones are there are in the number 800.

> Write

Draw a model of the number 800 using hundreds, tens and ones.

> Draw

CCSS.2.NBT.1.b

If you started at 0 and skip-counted by 100, would you say the number 510? **Write** yes or no. **Explain** your answer.

Write

Explain

Choose a number between 100 -1000. Write your number in base-ten numerals.

> Write

Write your number in expanded form.

> Write

Explain why it is important to read numbers, write numbers in base-ten numerals, and write numbers in expanded form.

Explain

_____

_____

_____

_____

_____

_____

CCSS.2.NBT.3

Draw a model of the number 902 using hundreds, tens, and ones.

Draw

Draw a model of the number 799 using hundreds, tens, and ones.

Draw

Write 902 and 799 with a symbol to show which number is greater.

Write

_____ ◯ _____

Explain how you know which number is greater.

Explain

_____

_____

_____

_____

CCSS.2.NBT.4

Write all of the strategies you have learned that help students learn their addition and subtraction facts. **Explain** which of these strategies works best for you.

Write

Explain

CCSS.2.NBT.5

Solve the equation: 23 + 41 + 59 + 42 = ? **Explain** one of the strategies you used to solve the equation.

Solve

Explain

_____

_____

_____

_____

_____

_____

_____

_____

Draw a model of 387 + 206 using hundreds, tens, and ones. **Solve** the problem.

Draw

Solve

Explain how to add 387 + 206 using hundreds, tens, and ones.

Explain

CCSS.2.NBT.7—A

© Common Core Education, Inc.

Draw a model of 708 - 615 using hundreds, tens, and ones. **Solve** the problem.

Draw

Solve

Explain how to add 708 - 615 using hundreds, tens, and ones.

Explain

_____

_____

_____

_____

_____

Write the number that is 10 more than 219.

> Write

Write the number that is 100 more than 417.

> Write

Write the number that is 10 more than 199.

> Write

Explain how you used mental math to get your answers.

Explain

_____

_____

_____

_____

_____

24
CCSS.1.NBT.8—A

Write the number that is 10 less than 520.

> Write

Write the number that is 10 less than 117.

> Write

Write the number that is 10 less than 407.

> Write

Explain how you used mental math to get your answers.

> **Explain**
>
> _____
>
> _____
>
> _____
>
> _____
>
> _____

Draw or write an example of the associative property of addition.

Draw **or** Write

Would this property work for subtraction? Write yes or no.

Write

_____

Explain your answer.

Explain

_____

_____

_____

_____

CCSS.2.NBT.9—A

Draw or write an example of the commutative property of addition.

> Draw or Write

Would this property work for subtraction? Write yes or no.

> Write
>
> _____

Explain your answer.

> **Explain**
>
> _____
>
> _____
>
> _____
>
> _____

Draw and **label** three tools used for measuring length.

┌───┐
│ Draw **and** Label   │
│   │
│   │
│   │
│   │
│   │
│   │
│   │
│   │
└───┘

Write an example of an object that could be measured with each tool.

┌───┐
│ Write   │
│   │
│ ─────────────────────────────────────── │
│   │
│ ─────────────────────────────────────── │
│   │
│ ─────────────────────────────────────── │
│   │
│ ─────────────────────────────────────── │
│   │
└───┘

CCSS.2.MD.1

Liza measured a window and found that it was 3 feet long. Jonelle measured the same window and found it was 36 inches long.

Explain why their answers are different.

Explain

_____

_____

_____

_____

_____

_____

_____

_____

_____

_____

_____

Draw two lines with different lengths using your centimeter ruler. Measure and label the length of each line.

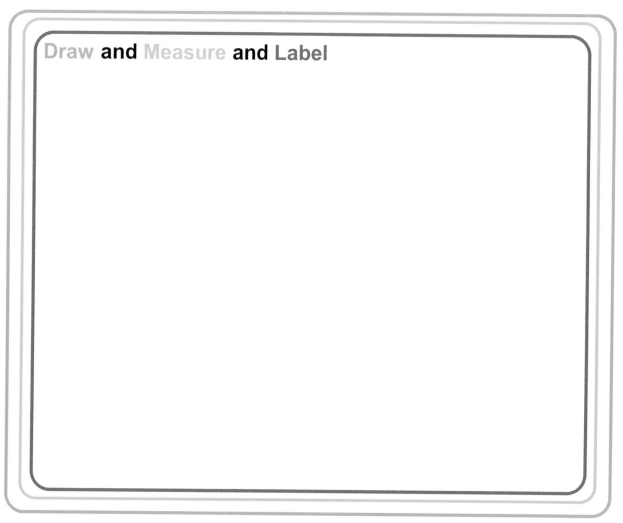

Draw and Measure and Label

Write and equation to find their difference in length. Solve the equation.

Write

Solve

CCSS.2.MD.4

Mari's goal is to swim 100 meters each day. Today she swam 78 meters and stopped. How many more meters does Mari need to swim today to meet her goal? Draw a picture. Write an equation. Use a ? for the unknown number. Solve this word problem.

Draw

Write

Solve

Draw and **label** a number line with points from 0 to 10. Draw on your number line to show the equation 9 - 3 = ?

Draw **and** Label

Explain how you got your answer.

Explain

CCSS.2.MD.6

Draw the hands on the clock to show 11:35 p.m. **Explain** how you got your answer using the words <u>hour hand</u> and <u>minute hand</u>.

Draw

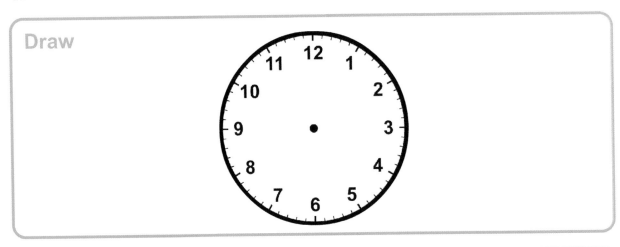

Explain

_____

_____

_____

_____

Write what you may be doing at 11:35 p.m.

Write

_____

Draw 2 quarters, 1 dime, 3 nickels, and 2 pennies. **Write** an equation to find the total amount of money. Use a ? for the unknown number. **Solve** this word problem.

Draw

Write

Solve

CCSS.2.MD.8

Kyle measured the length of ten pencils. Here is the data Kyle collected and recorded:

7 cm, 4 cm, 10 cm, 4 cm, 3 cm, 4cm, 8 cm, 7 cm, 5 cm, 10 cm

Draw a line plot to represent Kyle's data.

Draw

Write a sentence that tells something about Kyle's data.

Write

Type of Sticker	Number of Stickers
Happy Face	||||| |||
Star	||||| ||||| |||
Heart	||||| ||||| |||||
Flower	||

Draw and **label** a picture graph using the data from the table shown above.

Draw and **label**

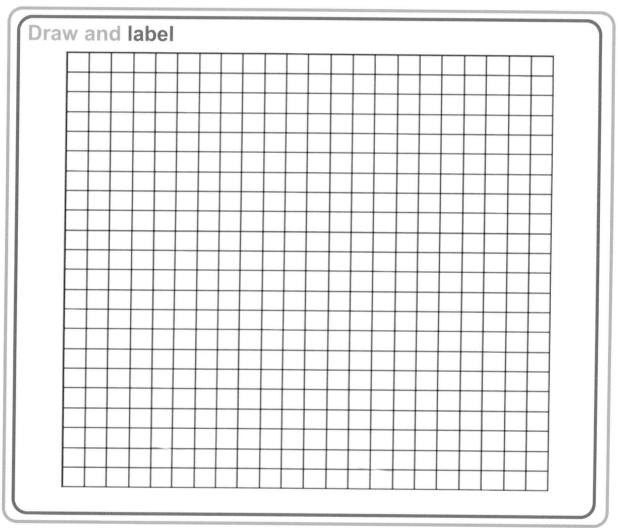

How many more heart stickers are there than flower stickers? **Solve** this word problem.

Solve

(This prompt is continued on the next page.)

© Common Core Education, Inc.

CCSS.2.MD.10—A

Draw and **label** a bar graph using the data from the same table shown on the left.

Draw and **label**

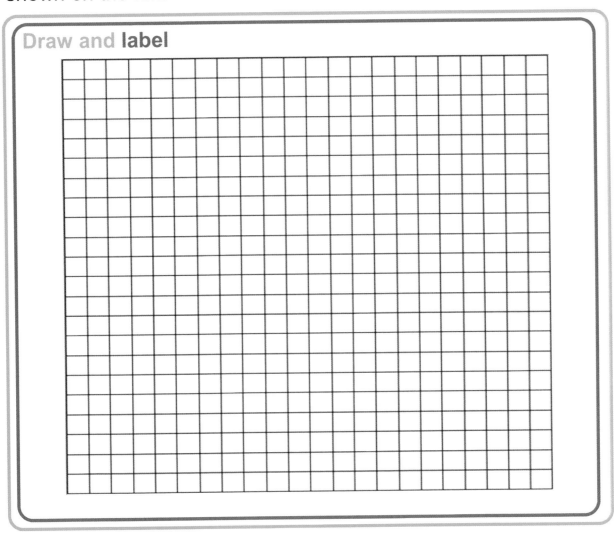

Write a question you can ask about the data using the words, <u>how many fewer</u>. **Solve** your word problem.

Write

_____

_____

Solve

Draw a quadrilateral.

Draw

Explain what makes it a quadrilateral.

Explain

CCSS.2.G.1—A

Draw a pentagon.

Draw

Explain what makes it a pentagon.

Explain

Draw a hexagon.

Draw

Explain what makes it a hexagon.

Explain

CCSS.2.G.1—C

Explain the difference between a two-dimensional shape and a three-dimensional shape.

Explain
_____
_____
_____
_____

Draw a cube.

Draw

Explain what makes it a cube.

Explain
_____
_____
_____
_____

Draw a rectangle that has a total of 12 squares. Write the number of rows and the number of columns in your rectangle.

Draw

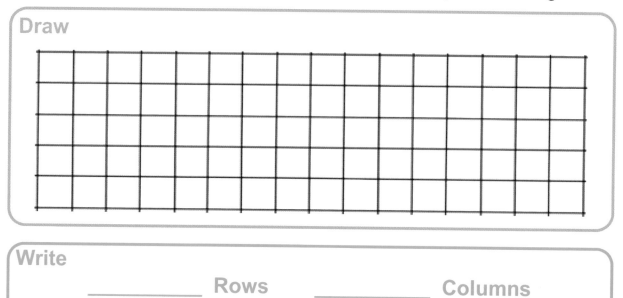

Write

_____ Rows   _____ Columns

Draw a different rectangle that has a total of 12 squares. Write the number of rows and the number of columns in your rectangle.

Draw

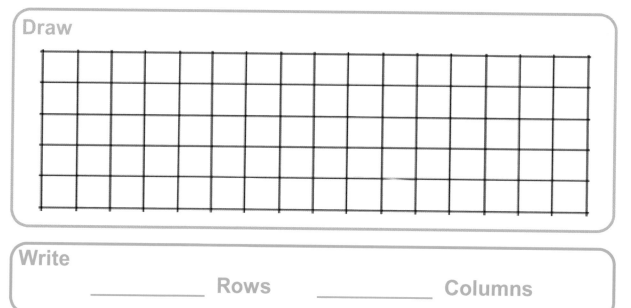

Write

_____ Rows   _____ Columns

(This prompt is continued on the next page.)

CCSS.2.G.2—A

Explain how the rectangles you drew are the same.

> **Explain**
>
> _____
>
> _____
>
> _____
>
> _____
>
> _____
>
> _____

Explain how these rectangles you drew are different.

> **Explain**
>
> _____
>
> _____
>
> _____
>
> _____
>
> _____
>
> _____

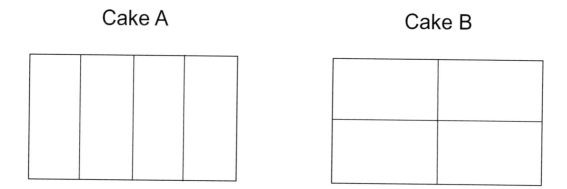

Cake A   Cake B

Ann had a fourth of Cake A. Sue had a fourth of Cake B. Ann said their shares are equal. Sue says their shares are not equal. Who is correct? **Explain** your answer.

Explain

CCSS.2.G.3

Content Vocabulary
Prompts

Addition

Draw a picture that shows **addition**. **Label** your picture.

Draw **and** Label

Explain what **addition** means.

Explain

Subtraction

Draw a picture that shows **subtraction**. Label your picture.

> **Draw and Label**

Explain what **subtraction** means.

> **Explain**

Equal

Draw an example using the **equal** sign. Write an equation that matches your drawing.

Draw

Write

Explain what **equal** means.

Explain

2.CV.3

Equation

Write an **equation** using the numbers 7, 15, 12.

Write

What is an **equation**? **Explain**.

Explain

Strategy

Write one math word problem **strategy** that you use.

Write

_____

_____

_____

Explain what the word **strategy** means.

Explain

_____

_____

_____

_____

_____

_____

_____

Data

Write an example of **data** you could collect in your class.

Write

What is an **data**? **Explain**.

Explain

Compare Numbers

Write and **label** the three symbols used to **compare numbers**.

> Write **and** Label

Explain how you would use each symbol to **compare numbers**.

> Explain

Length

Write the name of an item you could use to measure the **length** of your teacher's desk in <u>standard units</u>.

> **Write**
> _____

Write the name of a different item you could use to measure the **length** of your teacher's desk in <u>standard units</u>.

> **Write**
> _____

Explain what **length** means.

> **Explain**
> _____
> _____
> _____
> _____
> _____
> _____

Two-dimensional Shape

Draw an example of a **two-dimensional shape**.

Draw

What is a **two-dimensional shape**? Explain

Explain

2.CV.9

Three-dimensional Shape

Write the name of a **three-dimensional shape**.

Write

What is a **three-dimensional shape**? Explain.

Explain

Array

Draw an example of an **array**. Write an equation for your array.

Draw

Write

What is an **array**? Explain

Explain

Expanded Form

Write a three digit number in base-ten numerals.

> Write
>
> _____

Write the same number in **expanded form**.

> Write
>
>

What is **expanded form**? Explain.

> **Explain**
>
> _____
>
> _____
>
> _____
>
> _____
>
> _____
>
> _____
>
> _____

Self-Assessment

and

Peer Feedback

CCSS 2.OA.1   Page _____   Date _____

___ Self-assessment   ___ Peer Feedback (Name_____)

JUMPS:

_____

_____

BUMPS:

_____

_____

 My work shows that I understand   I made some mistakes, but I know how to fix them   I need help

---

CCSS 2.OA.2   Page _____   Date _____

___ Self-assessment   ___ Peer Feedback (Name_____)

JUMPS:

_____

_____

BUMPS:

_____

_____

My work shows that I understand   I made some mistakes, but I know how to fix them   I need help

CCSS 2.OA.3   Page _____   Date _____

___ Self-assessment   ___ Peer Feedback (Name_____)

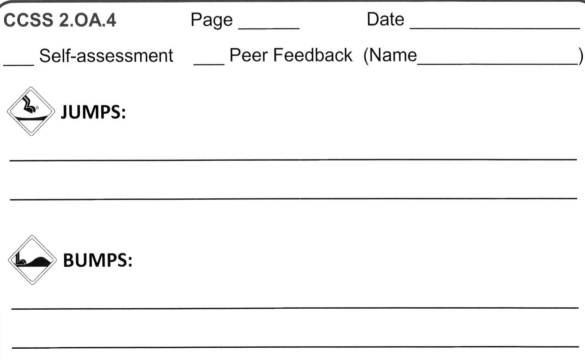 **JUMPS:**

_____

_____

BUMPS:

_____

_____

😊 **My work shows that I understand**   😐 I made some mistakes, but I know how to fix them   ☹ **I need help**

CCSS 2.OA.4   Page _____   Date _____

___ Self-assessment   ___ Peer Feedback (Name_____)

JUMPS:

_____

_____

BUMPS:

_____

_____

😊 **My work shows that I understand**   😐 I made some mistakes, but I know how to fix them   ☹ **I need help**

CCSS 2.NBT.1   Page _____   Date _____

___ Self-assessment   ___ Peer Feedback (Name_____)

JUMPS:

_____

_____

BUMPS:

_____

_____

😊 My work shows that I understand   😐 I made some mistakes, but I know how to fix them   🙁 I need help

---

CCSS 2.NBT.1.a   Page _____   Date _____

___ Self-assessment   ___ Peer Feedback (Name_____)

JUMPS:

_____

_____

BUMPS:

_____

_____

 My work shows that I understand   I made some mistakes, but I know how to fix them   I need help

CCSS 2.NBT.1.b   Page _____   Date _____

___ Self-assessment   ___ Peer Feedback (Name_____)

JUMPS:

_____

_____

BUMPS:

_____

_____

My work shows that I understand   I made some mistakes, but I know how to fix them   **I need help**

CCSS 2.NBT.2   Page _____   Date _____

___ Self-assessment   ___ Peer Feedback (Name_____)

JUMPS:

_____

_____

BUMPS:

_____

_____

My work shows that I understand   I made some mistakes, but I know how to fix them   **I need help**

CCSS 2.NBT.3

Page _____   Date _____

___ Self-assessment   ___ Peer Feedback (Name_____)

JUMPS:

_____

_____

BUMPS:

_____

_____

 My work shows that I understand   I made some mistakes, but I know how to fix them   I need help

---

CCSS 2.NBT.4

Page _____   Date _____

___ Self-assessment   ___ Peer Feedback (Name_____)

JUMPS:

_____

_____

BUMPS:

_____

_____

 My work shows that I understand   I made some mistakes, but I know how to fix them   I need help

CCSS 2.NBT.5   Page _____   Date _____

___ Self-assessment   ___ Peer Feedback (Name_____)

JUMPS:

_____

_____

BUMPS:

_____

_____

 My work shows that I understand   I made some mistakes, but I know how to fix them   **I need help**

CCSS 2.NBT.6   Page _____   Date _____

___ Self-assessment   ___ Peer Feedback (Name_____)

JUMPS:

_____

_____

BUMPS:

_____

_____

 My work shows that I understand   I made some mistakes, but I know how to fix them   **I need help**

CCSS 2.NBT.7

Page _____   Date _____

___ Self-assessment   ___ Peer Feedback (Name_____)

JUMPS:

_____

_____

BUMPS:

_____

_____

 My work shows that I understand   I made some mistakes, but I know how to fix them   I need help

---

CCSS 2.NBT.8

Page _____   Date _____

___ Self-assessment   ___ Peer Feedback (Name_____)

JUMPS:

_____

_____

BUMPS:

_____

_____

My work shows that I understand   I made some mistakes, but I know how to fix them   I need help

CCSS 2.NBT.9 Page _____ Date _____

___ Self-assessment ___ Peer Feedback (Name_____)

JUMPS:

_____

_____

BUMPS:

_____

_____

My work shows that I understand   I made some mistakes, but I know how to fix them   I need help

---

CCSS 2.MD.1 Page _____ Date _____

___ Self-assessment ___ Peer Feedback (Name_____)

JUMPS:

_____

_____

BUMPS:

_____

_____

My work shows that I understand   I made some mistakes, but I know how to fix them   I need help

CCSS 2.MD.2   Page _____   Date _____

___ Self-assessment   ___ Peer Feedback (Name_____)

JUMPS:

_____

_____

BUMPS:

_____

_____

 My work shows that I understand   I made some mistakes, but I know how to fix them   I need help

---

CCSS 2.MD.4   Page _____   Date _____

___ Self-assessment   ___ Peer Feedback (Name_____)

JUMPS:

_____

_____

BUMPS:

_____

_____

My work shows that I understand   I made some mistakes, but I know how to fix them   I need help

CCSS 2.MD.5   Page _____   Date _____

___ Self-assessment   ___ Peer Feedback (Name_____)

 JUMPS:

_____

_____

 BUMPS:

_____

_____

☺ **My work shows that I understand**   😐 **I made some mistakes, but I know how to fix them**   ☹ **I need help**

CCSS 2.MD.6   Page _____   Date _____

___ Self-assessment   ___ Peer Feedback (Name_____)

JUMPS:

_____

_____

BUMPS:

_____

_____

☺ **My work shows that I understand**   😐 **I made some mistakes, but I know how to fix them**   ☹ **I need help**

CCSS 2.MD.7   Page _____   Date _____

___ Self-assessment   ___ Peer Feedback (Name_____)

JUMPS:

_____

_____

BUMPS:

_____

_____

My work shows that I understand   I made some mistakes, but I know how to fix them   I need help

---

CCSS 2.MD.8   Page _____   Date _____

___ Self-assessment   ___ Peer Feedback (Name_____)

JUMPS:

_____

_____

BUMPS:

_____

_____

 My work shows that I understand   I made some mistakes, but I know how to fix them   I need help

Page _____   Date _____

___ Self-assessment   ___ Peer Feedback (Name_____)

JUMPS:

_____

_____

BUMPS:

_____

_____

My work shows that I understand   I made some mistakes, but I know how to fix them   I need help

---

Page _____   Date _____

___ Self-assessment   ___ Peer Feedback (Name_____)

JUMPS:

_____

_____

BUMPS:

_____

_____

My work shows that I understand   I made some mistakes, but I know how to fix them   I need help

CCSS 2.G.1   Page _____   Date _____

___ Self-assessment   ___ Peer Feedback (Name_____)

JUMPS:

_____

_____

BUMPS:

_____

_____

 My work shows that I understand   I made some mistakes, but I know how to fix them   I need help

---

CCSS 2.G.2   Page _____   Date _____

___ Self-assessment   ___ Peer Feedback (Name_____)

JUMPS:

_____

_____

BUMPS:

_____

_____

My work shows that I understand   I made some mistakes, but I know how to fix them   I need help

CCSS 2.G.3   Page _____   Date _____

___ Self-assessment   ___ Peer Feedback (Name_____)

JUMPS:

_____

_____

BUMPS:

_____

_____

My work shows that I understand

I made some mistakes, but I know how to fix them

I need help

CCSS 2.CV.1   Page _____   Date _____

___ Self-assessment   ___ Peer Feedback (Name_____)

JUMPS:

_____

_____

BUMPS:

_____

_____

My work shows that I understand

I made some mistakes, but I know how to fix them

I need help

CCSS 2.CV.2   Page _____   Date _____

___ Self-assessment   ___ Peer Feedback (Name_____)

 JUMPS:

_____

_____

 BUMPS:

_____

_____

 My work shows that I understand   I made some mistakes, but I know how to fix them   I need help

---

CCSS 2.CV.3   Page _____   Date _____

___ Self-assessment   ___ Peer Feedback (Name_____)

 JUMPS:

_____

_____

 BUMPS:

_____

_____

 My work shows that I understand   I made some mistakes, but I know how to fix them   I need help

74

CCSS 2.CV.4   Page _____   Date _____

___ Self-assessment   ___ Peer Feedback (Name_____)

JUMPS:

_____

_____

BUMPS:

_____

_____

My work shows that I understand   I made some mistakes, but I know how to fix them   I need help

---

CCSS 2.CV.5   Page _____   Date _____

___ Self-assessment   ___ Peer Feedback (Name_____)

JUMPS:

_____

_____

BUMPS:

_____

_____

My work shows that I understand   I made some mistakes, but I know how to fix them   I need help

CCSS 2.CV.6   Page _____   Date _____

___ Self-assessment   ___ Peer Feedback (Name_____)

JUMPS:

_____

_____

BUMPS:

_____

_____

:) My work shows that I understand   :| I made some mistakes, but I know how to fix them   :(I need help

---

CCSS 2.CV.7   Page _____   Date _____

___ Self-assessment   ___ Peer Feedback (Name_____)

JUMPS:

_____

_____

BUMPS:

_____

_____

:) My work shows that I understand   :| I made some mistakes, but I know how to fix them   :(I need help

CCSS 2.CV.8   Page _____   Date _____

___ Self-assessment   ___ Peer Feedback (Name_____)

 **JUMPS:**

_____

_____

 BUMPS:

_____

_____

 **My work shows that I understand**   **I made some mistakes, but I know how to fix them**   **I need help**

CCSS 2.CV.9   Page _____   Date _____

___ Self-assessment   ___ Peer Feedback (Name_____)

 **JUMPS:**

_____

_____

 BUMPS:

_____

_____

 **My work shows that I understand**   **I made some mistakes, but I know how to fix them**   **I need help**

© Common Core Education, Inc.

CCSS 2.CV.10

Page _____   Date _____

___ Self-assessment   ___ Peer Feedback (Name_____)

JUMPS:

_____

_____

BUMPS:

_____

_____

 My work shows that I understand   I made some mistakes, but I know how to fix them   **I need help**

CCSS 2.CV.11

Page _____   Date _____

___ Self-assessment   ___ Peer Feedback (Name_____)

JUMPS:

_____

_____

BUMPS:

_____

_____

 My work shows that I understand   I made some mistakes, but I know how to fix them   **I need help**

___ Self-assessment   ___ Peer Feedback (Name_____)

JUMPS:

_____

_____

BUMPS:

_____

_____

:) My work shows that I understand   :| I made some mistakes, but I know how to fix them   :(I need help

My Strategy Toolbox

Strategy Name: _____

What it looks like:

How this helps me solve problems:

_____

_____

_____

Tallies:

Strategy Name: _____

What it looks like:

How this helps me solve problems:

_____

_____

_____

Tallies:

Strategy Name: _____

What it looks like:

How this helps me solve problems:

_____

_____

_____

Tallies:

Strategy Name: _____

What it looks like:

How this helps me solve problems:

_____

_____

_____

Tallies:

Strategy Name: _____

What it looks like:

How this helps me solve problems:

_____

_____

_____

Tallies:

Strategy Name: _____

What it looks like:

How this helps me solve problems:

_____

_____

_____

Tallies:

Strategy Name: _____

What it looks like:

How this helps me solve problems:

_____

_____

_____

Tallies:

Strategy Name: _____

What it looks like:

How this helps me solve problems:

_____

_____

_____

Tallies:

Strategy Name: _____

What it looks like:

How this helps me solve problems:

_____

_____

_____

Tallies:

Strategy Name: _____

What it looks like:

How this helps me solve problems:

_____

_____

_____

Tallies:

Strategy Name: _____

What it looks like:

How this helps me solve problems:

_____

_____

_____

Tallies:

Strategy Name: _____

What it looks like:

How this helps me solve problems:

_____

_____

_____

Tallies:

Strategy Name: _____

What it looks like:

How this helps me solve problems:

_____

_____

_____

Tallies:

Strategy Name: _____

What it looks like:

How this helps me solve problems:

_____

_____

_____

Tallies:

Strategy Name: _____

What it looks like:

How this helps me solve problems:

_____

_____

_____

Tallies:

Strategy Name: _____

What it looks like:

How this helps me solve problems:

_____

_____

_____

Tallies:

Strategy Name: _____

What it looks like:

How this helps me solve problems:

_____

_____

_____

Tallies:

Strategy Name: _____

What it looks like:

How this helps me solve problems:

_____

_____

_____

Tallies:

Strategy Name: _____

What it looks like:

How this helps me solve problems:

_____

_____

_____

Tallies:

Strategy Name: _____

What it looks like:

How this helps me solve problems:

_____

_____

_____

Tallies:

Made in the USA
Charleston, SC
13 July 2016